AF428700

Interlude

The Heart Echo
In the stillness of a quiet room,
The heart hums its tender tune.
An echo, soft but sure,
Whispers of the love it bore.
Through every beat, a story told,
Of moments cherished, brave and bold.
Of dreams once sparked, now grown,
In the heart, the seeds are sown.
But echoes are not merely past—
They carry forward, they will last.
A ripple through the air, they glide,
A map of what we feel inside.
For every ache, a song remains,
Every joy, a sweet refrain.
The heart's echo, never lost,
Reminds us love is worth the cost.

Dedications

To everyone who has faced the silent battles of mental illness,
To those who carry the weight of everyday struggles, yet rise again,
This collection is for you.
May these words echo your strength, your resilience, and your
courage.
You are not alone.
With love and understanding,

Dalila Love

A Poetry and Journal Guide

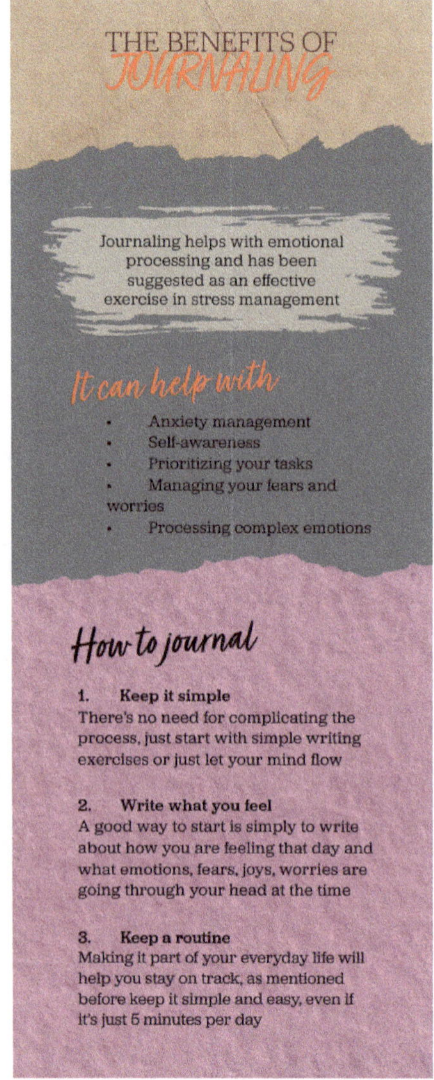

I

Down Below

I'm Sinking Again
And My Feet Are Chained

The Lack Of Oxygen Is Causing The Color
From My Face To Drain

Although I'm Scared
I Can't Complain

Because I Know I'll No Longer Be In Pain

Psalm 34:18 (NIV):
"The Lord is close to the brokenhearted and saves those who are
crushed in spirit."

JOURNAL ENTRY

Name:

Date:

II

Breaking The Cycle

They say the abused become the abuser
But I don't see that in my future

And I wish to be nothing like you
I didn't grow up with a silver spoon

But whose to say my children won't
And when they feel like giving up

I'll be there to make sure they don't.

Isaiah 41:10 (NIV):
"So do not fear, for I am with you; do not be dismayed, for I am your God. I will strengthen you and help you; I will uphold you with my righteous right hand."

JOURNAL ENTRY

Name:

Date:

III

Affections

If you wish to gain my attention
then you should act with intentions

I crave deep connections
and I despise surface-level attractions

Your words mean nothing without action

Your lust is not wanted or needed
But your efforts are seen and appreciated.

1 John 3:18 (NIV):
"Dear children, let us not love with words or speech but with actions and in
truth."

JOURNAL ENTRY

Name:

Date:

IV

Disconnected

You've changed

Yeah you would too
if you watched the light fade from your own eyes

Your closest friends walk away from you because you're too depressed

Your family looks at you as if you're a stranger

You look in the mirror and feel repulsed by your own reflection
And the only feeling you feel is anger.

Psalm 88:18 (NIV):
"You have taken from me friend and neighbor—darkness is my closest
friend."

JOURNAL ENTRY

Name:

Date:

V

Come As You Are

I never understood the misconception that people are ugly

I could never just look at a person and perceive them as ugly

*I feel as though if you judge a person by their looks
you yourself are an ugly person.*

1 Samuel 16:7 (NIV):
*"The Lord does not look at the things people look at. People look at the out-
ward appearance, but the Lord looks at the heart."*

JOURNAL ENTRY

Name:

Date:

VI

❦

Wishful Thinking

I can only hope
that I'm allowed through the threshold called heaven

The place of love and the awakened

or am I forced to stay in the dark with the dead and unforgiven?

John 5:24 (NIV):
"Very truly I tell you, whoever hears my word and believes him who sent me has eternal life and will not be judged but has crossed over from death to life."

JOURNAL ENTRY

Name:

Date:

VII

The Hands

You left my body bruised and battered

I asked you to stop
Not that it mattered

Days passed even weeks
and my world still seems so bleak

Everything you did is on repeat in my head
Giving me another reason to wish that I was dead.

Psalm 147:3 (NIV):
"He heals the brokenhearted and binds up their wounds."

JOURNAL ENTRY

Name:

Date:

VIII

Please Be Mines

The moment her lips touched mine
our souls entwined

All I could taste was cherry wine
the expensive kind

She refused to tell me her name
I wonder why

She is in her own category
one that could not be defined

When I'm with her I feel a special kind of high
and when I look into her eyes my feelings amplify
She made my world stir with emotions I didn't know could occur.

Song of Solomon 4:10 (NIV):
"How delightful is your love, my sister, my bride! How much more pleasing
is your love than wine, and the fragrance of your perfume more than any
spice!"

JOURNAL ENTRY

Name:

Date:

IX

Never Again

I've become weary of who I let in

Afraid I'm going to make the same mistakes once more

All it takes is a misjudge of character

And I'm spiraling out of control again.

Proverbs 4:23 (NIV):
"Above all else, guard your heart, for everything you do flows from it."

JOURNAL ENTRY

Name:

Date:

X

He Guides Me

I'm stuck in this dream state of never-ending loneliness

Walking this path of unhappiness
shrouded by darkness

Looking for my soul that was taken from me
while asking for forgiveness

I cry to him my lord and savior
my witness

He guides me back home
and tells me this is where I belong

I realized my soul was never gone it was with me all along.

Isaiah 58:11 (NIV):
"The Lord will guide you always; he will satisfy your needs in a sun-scorched land and will strengthen your frame. You will be like a well-watered garden, like a spring whose waters never fail."

JOURNAL ENTRY

Name:

Date:

XI

Until We Meet Again

They say people come and go
I still remember our first hello

I ask god why it had to be you
Could it have been for the best
I never liked checkers or chest

But navigating your heart was like a board game
A game I never grew bored of

The love we had for each other was unrivaled

I'm trying to keep a leveled head
But I really wish it was me instead

I would do anything to see my angel again.

Revelation 21:4 (NIV):
"'He will wipe every tear from their eyes. There will be no more death' or mourning or crying or pain, for the old order of things has passed away."

JOURNAL ENTRY

Name:

Date:

XII

Unrequited Love

Unrequited love is the love that makes you question why not me

The love that makes you physically weak

The love that has you tossing and turning in your sleep
The love that makes you cry and weep

The love that makes you loose your sanity

The love that doesn't grant you the courtesy
The love that burns you like a 3rd degree

The love that makes you wait and see
The love that no one wants to be.

Proverbs 13:12 (NIV):
"Hope deferred makes the heart sick, but a longing fulfilled is a tree of life."

JOURNAL ENTRY

Name:

Date:

XIII

I'll Be Okay Without You

You never had the heart to show me the real you
And when the truth came out
I knew that was my cue

Call me gone girl
because I'm never coming back

And I know you are mad
because he's everything that you lack

I'll never give you the satisfaction of seeing me cry
I wish you the best but this is goodbye.

Isaiah 43:18-19 (NIV):
"Forget the former things; do not dwell on the past. See, I am doing a new thing! Now it springs up; do you not perceive it? I am making a way in the wilderness and streams in the wasteland."

JOURNAL ENTRY

Name:

Date:

XV

Exceptionally You

They call us outcasts

I say we're just drifters

Looking for a place

that knows no bounds.

1 Peter 2:9 (NIV):
"But you are a chosen people, a royal priesthood, a holy nation, God's special possession, that you may declare the praises of him who called you out of darkness into his wonderful light."

JOURNAL ENTRY

Name:

Date:

XVI

Unchosen

If you were put into a room with me

Would you have noticed me then

Or would you look right past me

Because I'll never be them.

Luke 12:7 (NIV):
"Indeed, the very hairs of your head are all numbered. Don't be afraid; you are worth more than many sparrows."

JOURNAL ENTRY

Name:

Date:

XVII

Abandoned

You left me you might as well say you abandoned ship

Leaving without a goodbye
and when you see me I can't even get a simple hi

This is deep so deep
not even the human eye can pry

I wish I understood why
that's going to linger on my mind

Now when I think of you
all I can do is cry

It doesn't matter how many questions I have on the inside
Because you'll never care to explain why.

Psalm 34:18 (NIV):
"The Lord is close to the brokenhearted and saves those who are crushed in
spirit."

JOURNAL ENTRY

Name:

Date:

XVIII

Wanderer

Sometimes I'm here and
sometimes I'm not

I get stuck in between reality
and fantasy

I wander around aimlessly
not knowing my destiny

I tell myself it'll be ok
but then I'm away for more than I can take

I begin to fall into oblivion
Until my heart beats again

I've come to realize it's too late and now my new world awaits.

Jeremiah 29:11 (NIV):
*"For I know the plans I have for you," declares the Lord, "plans to prosper
you and not to harm you, plans to give you hope and a future."*

JOURNAL ENTRY

Name:

Date:

XIX

Melodramatic

You're allowed to feel it's what makes us human

But what happens when you feel too much

Every emotion you feel is felt through great detail

So great that you can't control it

And you wish others understood this

Unfortunately, they don't and they never will.

Psalm 56:8 (NIV):
"Record my misery; list my tears on your scroll—are they not in your record?"

JOURNAL ENTRY

Name:

Date:

XX

Oddball

What an odd number you are 7

But you're not alone

At least you have 11.

Ecclesiastes 4:9-10 (NIV):
"Two are better than one, because they have a good return for their labor: If either of them falls down, one can help the other up. But pity anyone who falls and has no one to help them."

JOURNAL ENTRY

Name:

Date:

XXI

Distasteful

Truth of the matter is

I don't find anyone appealing

I'm appalled by the slightest bit of affection

I try to stay away from people that cause tension

But that's proving to be quite challenging despite my proposition.

Proverbs 13:20 (NIV):
"Walk with the wise and become wise, for a companion of fools suffers harm."

JOURNAL ENTRY

Name:

Date:

XXII

Unseen

If I was an emotion
it would be greed

Because I'll do anything
Just to be seen.

James 4:2 (NIV):
"You desire but do not have, so you kill. You covet but you cannot get what
you want, so you quarrel and fight. You do not have because you do not ask
God."

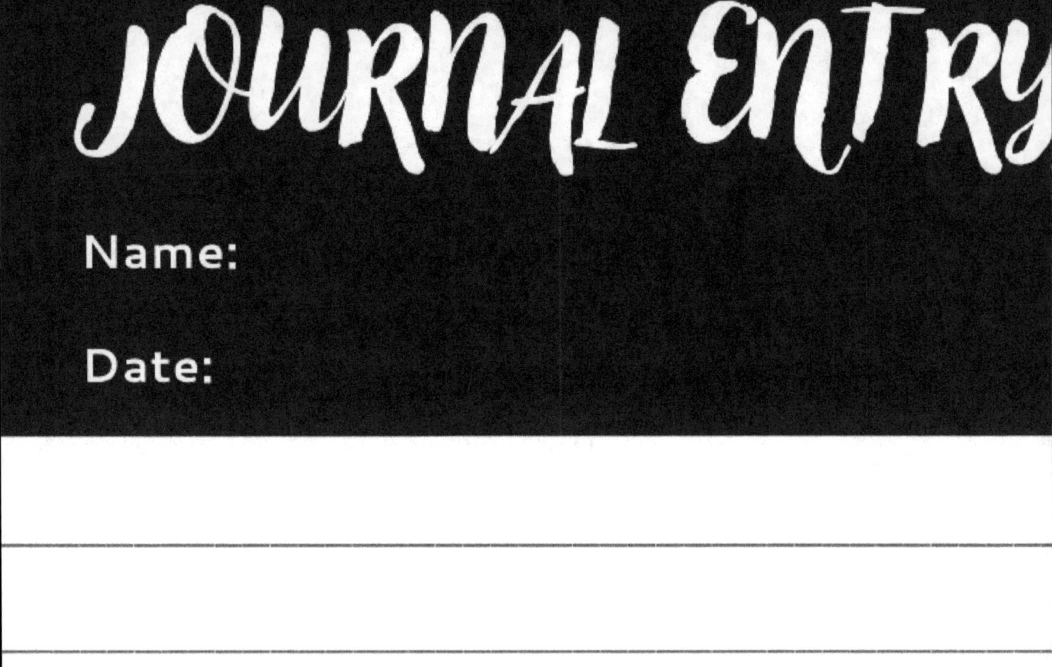

JOURNAL ENTRY

Name:

Date:

XXIII

The Voices

Even in a world full of pain they still call my name

Telling me I should pick up my favorite blade

I press deep into my flesh
and let my worries fade away

And then the only feeling I'm left with is shame

Because I know people won't look at me the same

And at the end of the day
the voices are all I have to blame.

Psalm 147:3 (NIV):
"He heals the brokenhearted and binds up their wounds."

JOURNAL ENTRY

Name:

Date:

XXIV

Bittersweet

I'm tired of being treated like a free trial

People like to test me out

but when it's time to pay they disappear

And then it's like they were never here.

Matthew 7:6 (NIV):
"Do not give dogs what is sacred; do not throw your pearls to pigs. If you do, they may trample them under their feet, and then turn and tear you to pieces."

JOURNAL ENTRY

Name:

Date:

Dalila Love is a passionate young writer whose love for reading and poetry blossomed in her adolescence. Having faced the challenges of mental illness, Dalila sought to transform her experiences into words, creating a collection that resonates with the pain and triumphs of the human spirit. The Heart Echo is her heartfelt attempt to connect with others through poetry, offering solace and understanding to those who find themselves navigating similar struggles. With each verse, Dalila invites readers into her world, sharing not just her journey but also the universal emotions that bind us all together.